THE ADVENT INSTRUCTOR

Reflections On Christmas Symbolism

KENNETH A. MORTONSON

CSS Publishing Company, Inc.
Lima, Ohio

THE ADVENT INSTRUCTOR

Scripture quotations are from the *Revised Standard Version of the Bible,* copyright-
ed 1946, 1952 (c), 1971, 1973, by the Division of Christian Education of the National
Council of the Churches of Christ in the USA. Used by permission.

Library of Congress Cataloging-in-Publication Data

Mortonson, Kenneth, 1927-
    The Advent instructor : reflections on Christmas symbolism / Kenneth A. Mor-
tonson.
        p.   cm.
    Includes bibliographical references and index.
    ISBN 0-7880-0562-6
    1. Advent. 2. Christian art and symbolism. 3. Christmas. I. Title.
BV40.M68   1995
263'.91—dc20   95-12296
                                                                          CIP

ISBN: 0-7880-0562-6
PRINTED IN U.S.A.

"The trouble with some of us is that we have been inoculated with small doses of Christianity which keep us from catching the real thing." — Leslie Dixon Weatherhead

"I will honor Christmas in my heart and try to keep it all the year." — Ebeneezer Scrooge in *A Christmas Carol* by Charles Dickens

"This is the message we have heard from him and proclaim to you, that God is light and in him is no darkness at all. If we say we have fellowship with him while we walk in darkness, we lie and do not live according to the truth; but if we walk in the light, as he is in the light, we have fellowship with one another, and the blood of Jesus his Son cleanses us from all sin." — 1 John 1:5-7

Table Of Contents

Introduction

The approach of the Christmas season is a time when the yearly routine of life often changes. Even before Thanksgiving is past, we begin to see the signs of the approaching holiday. It is interesting to remember that the term *holiday* has its origin in the idea of a "holy day." A basic meaning of holy is that which is set apart; that which is different from the ordinary. Thus, a holy day or "holiday" is meant to be a time set apart for a specific remembrance or celebration. It is a time that is marked by differences when compared to the ordinary days of life.

Christmas, however, is more than a day; it is a season. The season before the day is called *Advent.* This is a religious term that refers to having a season of preparation for a special, holy day. Therefore, the time prior to the actual day of Christmas has become a season that is filled with many special things; not the least of which is the symbolism of Christmas.

The length of the Advent season will vary from year to year. It is generally described as "the Sunday nearest Saint Andrew's Day," which is November 30th. It ends on Christmas Eve. Most of the time, the season will begin with the first Sunday after Thanksgiving. However, when there are five Thursdays in November, Advent will begin with the first Sunday in December. Therefore, the number of days in Advent may vary from 22 to 28 days. With that in mind, I have provided a total of 28 separate items for reflection in addition to this introduction.

With each reflection, you will find a brief explanation of a symbol or a symbolic person, plus some suggested thoughts on how the image may be used to instruct us in the Christian faith. You will also find a verse or two from the songs and poems of the season that may add to your understanding of the meditation.

Too often we look at things and fail to think about what they can mean to us. Life is full of symbols. In fact, what you are doing right now depends upon the use of symbols and the understanding of what these symbols represent as you read the printed page. Your reflection upon the meaning of the words read is called learning. The application of that learning to life is called wisdom.

Paul reminds us of the need to understand the symbolic meaning of words when he wrote, "There are doubtless many different languages in the world, and none is without meaning; but if I do not know the meaning of the language, I shall be a foreigner to the speaker and the speaker a foreigner to me. So with yourselves; since you are eager for manifestations of the Spirit, strive to excel in building up the church" (1 Corinthians 14:10-12).

The same thing can be said about being able to understand the symbols of the Advent season. The more we understand the symbolic meanings, the more we will be able to strengthen ourselves, and others, in the faith.

In 1906, Helen Keller was quoted in the December issue of *Ladies' Home Journal* as saying, "The only real blind person at Christmas is he who has not Christmas in his heart."

The Advent season is a special time of the year when the change in routine can bring great stress or great joy. In reality, it is usually a mixture of both. May this meditative book help you to see new meaning in the symbols of the season and may the new meanings strengthen your faith, add to your inner peace and give new vitality to your faith.

Kenneth Mortonson
Macomb, Illinois

The Color Purple

.The church year is filled with special annual festivals, or high days. Two of the major times, of course, are Christmas and Easter which mark the beginning and the fulfillment of the life and ministry of Jesus. In the early years of the church, a period of time before each celebration was set aside as a time to prepare for it. The time before Easter is called Lent and this period preceding Christmas is Advent. Lent originally meant "spring" and Advent means "coming."

Throughout the Church year, various colors are used to help mark the special seasons. We shall look again at some of the special Christmas season colors, but for now, a quick review of the meaning of the colors might be helpful. Symbolism goes beyond shapes; therefore, if a person is to find meaning in the Advent season, it is important to remember that even the color that is used has a special meaning. Green is the color of vegetation and, therefore, of growth. In the spring, things begin to grow and so the green color reminds us of the triumph of spring over winter, of life over death. Red is the color of blood and is used in the seasons that remember the martyred believers. Red also symbolizes fire and is used during Pentecost. White is used to symbolize purity and holiness. Gold is the color of wealth and precious things. It is also a symbol for divinity and sacredness. Purple has two meanings. It is the color of royalty and, therefore, is a sign of imperial power. But purple is also the color of sorrow and penitence and in that sense is used in the season of preparation for Christmas (Advent) and for Easter (Lent). Part of our preparation for the celebration of what God has done for us is to remember our need of God and his Christ. We need to acknowledge our imperfections so that we can seek better things. We need to confess that we cannot save ourselves so that we will be open to God's salvation in Jesus. We need Jesus, the mediator. "For there is one God, and there is one mediator between God and men, the man Christ Jesus, who gave himself as a ransom for all, the testimony to which was borne at the proper time" (1 Timothy 2:5, 6).

This world-changing event — the coming of God's Mediator — began with the birth of the Christ child. The period of self-preparation for understanding what that event means is Advent. And so the calendar of the Christian year begins with the first day of Advent. It is a time of opportunity, a time to capture anew the true spirit of the season and of the day. Think about it.

> *O come, O come, Emmanuel,*
> *And ransom captive Israel,*
> *That mourns in lonely exile here*
> *Until the Son of God appear.*
> *Rejoice! Rejoice!*
> *Emmanuel Shall come to thee, O Israel.*
>
> (12th Century Latin. Translated by John Mason Neale, 1851)

Wreaths

The word *wreath* refers to an object that is made by turning and bending material to form a circular object. It is often used as a decoration, as we see in the Advent season. It has also been worn on the head, in special periods of history, as a type of crown. When Jesus was crucified, they placed a crown of thorns upon his head because he was called the "King of the Jews." That crown was a wreath of thorn-covered branches woven in a circle. Another common use of the wreath today is as a grave decoration as a kind of memorial.

The unique feature of the wreath is that it is in the form of a circle and therein lies its significance. No matter how beautiful it might be or how much people may misuse it as an instrument of torture, it stands before us as a symbol of eternity. The circle, once constructed, has no beginning and no end. "For God so loved the world that he gave his only Son, that whoever believes in him shall not perish but have eternal life. For God sent the Son into the world, not to condemn the world, but that the world might be saved through him" (John 3:16, 17). In the book of the Revelation of John, Jesus is reported as saying, "I am the Alpha and the Omega" (Revelation 1:8). Alpha and Omega are the first and last letters of the Greek alphabet. The words symbolize the beginning and the end; the completeness of what Jesus is and what he means to the totality of life.

In the season of Advent, as we prepare to remember the wonderful gift given to us by God, the Father, whenever we see that symbol of the circle let us remember we are celebrating things that shall influence us and our world forever. And when our time comes to quit this world, the eternal truths of our faith shall still influence us. Think about it.

13

Be near me, Lord Jesus; I ask Thee to stay
Close by me forever, and love me, I pray.
Bless all the dear children in Thy tender care,
And fit us for heaven to live with Thee there.

(From "Away In A Manger," attributed to
Martin Luther. Some sources indicate that
John Thomas McFarland was the author of
this third stanza.)

Evergreens

The wreath is not the only symbol that we use in the Advent season to remind us about the things of eternity. The evergreen, which is often woven into a wreath or used as the holder of so many different ornaments (which can be symbols of the elements of Christmas and its meaning), is a symbol whose name points to its meaning: "ever green." For ever and ever speaks again of the eternal. Green is the symbol of life. When the deciduous trees are growing, their branches are covered with green leaves. If the tree dies for some reason, the leaves either fall off early or do not develop in the spring. In the fall, when the tree becomes dormant — like unto death — the leaves fall. In that dormant period, there is very little growth. When the green leaves arrive in the spring, the tree's vitality returns and it grows. Green is the symbol of life. To be alive is to keep on growing and producing the fruit of life.

In our faith, we can believe that we shall be ever green, ever growing as we live eternally with God. Jesus told his disciples, and through them he told us, "And this is eternal life, that they know thee the only true God, and Jesus Christ whom thou (God, the Father) hast sent" (John 17:3). The author of Hebrews also pointed to our need to continue to move toward maturity in the faith, our need to keep on growing, when he wrote, "For though by this time you ought to be teachers, you need some one to teach you again the first principles of God's word. You need milk, not solid food; for every one who lives on milk is unskilled in the word of righteousness, for he is a child. But solid food is for the mature, for those who have their faculties trained by practice to distinguish good from evil" (Hebrews 5:12-14). Paul, in Ephesians, wrote of our need to grow up into Christ. "Speaking the truth in love, we are to

15

grow up in every way into him who is the head, into Christ, from whom the whole body, joined and knit together by every joint with which it is supplied, when each part is working properly, makes bodily growth and upbuilds itself in love" (Ephesians 4:15-16). Think about it.

> *Good Christian men, rejoice With heart and soul and voice;*
> *Now ye need not fear the grave: Peace! Peace! Jesus Christ was born to save!*
> *Calls you one and calls you all To gain his everlasting hall.*
> *Christ was born to save! Christ was born to save!*

> (Latin carol, translated by John M. Neale, 1853)

The Symbol
Of The Lights

One of the major symbols of Christmas is the Christmas tree lights. Before the time of electricity, the decorated evergreen tree often had lighted candles as an important part of the tree's adornment. Today, the candle has been replaced by the light bulb and its beauty is applied to houses and outdoor trees and bushes, and to wood and wire forms.

The symbolism of light is at the heart of the Christian faith. John pointed out early in his gospel that "In him (Jesus) was life, and the life was the light of men. The light shines in the darkness, and the darkness has not overcome it" (John 1:4, 5). Jesus spoke of himself as the light of the world. "I am the light of the world; he who follows me will not walk in darkness, but will have the light of life" (John 8:12). It is our faith that if we want to know how life is to be lived as God intended it to be, then we need to see life in the light of Jesus' life and teachings.

The colored lights remind us of the variety of wonderful things that we have in life. The abundance of light in this season speaks to the abundant life offered in Jesus. He taught, "I came that they may have life, and have it abundantly" (John 10:10).

The Old Testament also used the symbol of light to help us understand what God has given to us. In the longest chapter in the Bible, the Psalmist reminds us, in speaking of God, "Thy word is a lamp to my feet and a light to my path" (Psalm 119:105). To walk in darkness is a frightening experience, especially when you are walking through new territory. Life becomes easier when you can see where you are going or if you have found a way of living that helps you to know where and how you should go. The word of God is a guide to living the one true life and Jesus is the Word that "became flesh and dwelt among us, full of grace and truth; we have beheld his glory, glory as of the only Son from the Father" (John 1:14). Think about it.

> *O Christmas Tree, O Christmas Tree,*
> *Thy beauty doth remind us,*
> *Though hearts were filled with joy and mirth*
> *Today we hail the Savior's birth.*
> *O Christmas Tree, O Christmas Tree.*
> *Thy beauty doth remind us.*

> (From an old German carol, "O Tan-nenbaum")

The Power
Of The Lights

As we have seen, lights glowing on the Christmas tree or as part of the outdoor decorations are a major part of the beauty of the season. In order for the lights to work three things are needed: the light bulb, a source of power and wires to carry the electricity to the light bulb. When you have all three and the proper connections are made, then you can light up. But if any one of these three parts is missing, or not working properly, the light will go out.

A similar condition exists in our spiritual life. If we are to be aware of the presence of God in life three things are also needed. First, we must accept the fact that we are not perfect. We need forgiveness. "If we say we have no sin, we deceive ourselves, and the truth is not in us. If we confess our sins, he is faithful and just, and will forgive our sins and cleanse us from all unrighteousness" (1 John 1:8, 9). "If we walk in the light, as he is in the light, we have fellowship with one another, and the blood of Jesus his Son cleanses us from all sin" (1 John 1:7).

We cannot save ourselves; just as the light bulb cannot light itself. When we are willing to accept forgiveness then we are ready to be lighted. God is the source of that salvation, that power. Acknowledging this brings the second needed element — power — into the picture.

The third essential is the connection between that power and our need, and that connection is Jesus. "For there is one God, and there is one mediator between God and men, the man Christ Jesus" (1 Timothy 2:5).

Once God has entered our life, we can experience what Jesus meant when he said, "You are the light of the world ... Let your light so shine before men, that they may see

19

your good works and give glory to your Father who is in heaven" (Matthew 5:14, 16). When the current enters the light bulb, and the light is as it should be, it will shine. Think about it.

O one with God the Father in majesty and might,
The Brightness of His glory, Eternal Light of light,
O'er this our home of darkness Thy rays are streaming
*   now;*
The shadows flee before Thee; the world's true Light
*   are Thou.*

(By William Walsham How, 1871)

The Candle

Though the candle is not used today as a light on the Christmas tree, it is still an important symbol of the season. In many windows an electric light is seen, as a candle, sending forth its light to guide people home. In Ireland, the lighted candle in the window was part of their tradition that said "welcome" to priest or passerby.

While the electric candle never changes its shape, we need to remember the meaning of the real candle. When not with flame, it stands ever ready to be lighted. The candle exists for that purpose. And when it is lighted, the real candle continues to burn, with its soft light, until the candle is consumed.

Here is a constant reminder that many things in life find their meaning in the act of giving. The candle, for example, was invented to give. If it did not give light, it would not exist. This symbol is, therefore, one that points to a basic Christian idea: namely, that in giving we receive the blessings of life. Luke reminds us of Paul's words, in Acts 20:35, that Jesus said, "It is more blessed to give than to receive." One reason for this is that we are called to be a servant people. A servant is one who stands ever ready to help the people he or she serves. Jesus taught his disciples, "Truly, truly, I say to you, a servant is not greater than his master, nor is he who is sent greater than he who sent him. If you know these things, blessed are you if you do them" (John 13:16, 17). Notice that when Jesus says, "Truly, truly," it is a sign to the listener that he is saying something very important. It is the same as on a navy ship when the order is given, "Now hear this!"

As we celebrate the coming of Jesus, we must not forget his own words that "the Son of man came not to be served, but to serve" (Matthew 20:28). Think about it.

21

Love came down at Christmas, Love all lovely, Love divine;
Love was born at Christmas, Stars and angels gave the sign.

Worship we the Godhead, Love incarnate, Love divine;
Worship we our Jesus: But wherewith for sacred sign?

Love shall be our token, Love be yours and love be mine,
Love to God and all men, Love for plea and gift and sign.

(By Christina G. Rossetti 1830-1894)

Homemade Gifts

An element of continuity with the past is to be found in the practice of making gifts to be given at Christmas time. We call this the heritage of folk art. Long before this country became a nation, and for many decades after, the people in the new colonies used their special skills to make their own gifts and decorations for Christmas. There were no supermarkets or catalog houses from which to obtain items for giving. Most of the material things they possessed were handmade. In those days, for example, sewing was a necessity, and not just a hobby. Mothers oversaw the making of samplers to teach numbers and letters, as well as to give practice in the art of sewing. Therefore, in the season before Christmas, using whatever was available, they put their skills to good use as they made useful gifts for the other members of the family.

There is something special about a homemade gift. In the giving, the person presents not just a gift, but the uniqueness of the giver whose skills made the creation. Often, many hours of time were spent in the creation of the object, so — in a sense — the giver gives some of the self in that gift.

Such gifts remind us of God's gift in Christ Jesus. As Paul expressed it, "Have this mind among yourselves, which you have in Christ Jesus, who, though he was in the form of God, did not count equality with God a thing to be grasped, but emptied himself, taking the form of a servant, being born in the likeness of men" (Philippians 2:5-7). God in Christ came in human form to personally express his love for us. Whenever we find a way to give of ourselves to another we are reflecting the love of God.

Jesus was the incarnation of God. "The Word became flesh and dwelt among us, full of grace and truth; we have beheld his glory, glory as of the only Son from the Father'' (John 1:14). Our mission, as Christians, is to take that Spirit of love and caring and embody it in the way we live. Think about it.

Yea, Lord, we greet Thee, Born this happy morning,
O Jesus, to Thee be all glory given;
Word of the Father, Now in flesh appearing!
O come, let us adore Him, O come let us adore Him!
O come, let us adore Him, Christ the Lord!

("O Come, All Ye Faithful" 18th Century
Latin, translated by Frederick Oakeley, 1841)

The Christmas Cookies

Perhaps no homemade items are more abundant at this season of the year than the Christmas cookies. They come in all colors, sizes and shapes from the cut-out Christmas tree cookies to the many layered bar cookies. They are fun to make and even young children can become involved in helping with the stirring and decorating. Imagine the thrill for a youngster who can hand the decorated plate of cookies to a family friend and say, "I helped make these!"

As you look at the final product from your kitchen, as the variety of cookies fills the platter, pause for a moment to reflect upon what that sight represents. All the objects, taken together, can be labelled "cookies." Yet, each is unique in size and shape, and between groups of cookies there are a variety of flavors. The recipient of your gift will have added joy in the experience of tasting your well-chosen selections.

I would suggest that this variety in creation is akin to what God has done with the human race. He has created each person uniquely. We are all different. We come in different sizes and colors. We are born with distinctive features and appearances. God's mosaic is beautiful to behold. As Paul instructed, "Now there are varieties of gifts, but the same Spirit; and there are varieties of service, but the same Lord; and there are varieties of working, but it is the same God who inspires them all in every one. To each is given the manifestation of the Spirit for the common good" (1 Corinthians 12:4-7).

In order for our individuality to make its special contribution to the life of God's world, it is essential that we look to our personal relationships with God in Christ Jesus. The direction for life is not to be found simply by watching the people around us and striving to mock what we see there. It is not to be found by trying to be like everyone else. Jesus taught his disciples saying, "Do not judge by appearances, but judge with right judgment" (John 7:24). Part of that right judgment for the Christian is to strive to live in a right relationship with God. As Jesus said, "Seek first his kingdom and his righteousness, and all these things shall be yours as well" (Matthew 6:33). You cannot make your special contribution to God's purpose until you become that unique person God intended you to be. Think about it.

Take my hands, and let them move At the impulse of Thy love.
Take my feet, and let them be Swift and beautiful for Thee.
Take my silver and my gold; Not a mite would I withhold.
Take my intellect, and use Every power as Thou shalt choose.
Take my love; my Lord, I pour At Thy feet its treasure store.
Take myself, and I will be Ever, only, all for Thee.

(From "Take My Life" by Frances Ridley Havergal 1836-1879)

Santa Claus

For many people, Santa Claus is viewed as a symbol of the secular world. The jolly old man, in a bright red suit, goes around asking children what they want for Christmas. Department stores hire a "Santa's Helper" to extract from the little ones a list of things the store hopes their parents will buy while in their halls of commerce. How can we find any religious meaning in a symbol that seems to center on encouraging children to think of material things?

First, remember that "Santa Claus" has a religious origin in Saint Nicholas. He was born in Patras, a city of Lycia, in Asia Minor nearly 300 years after the birth of Christ. In time, he became a bishop and the patron saint of children. Without going into all the details of his life, for our purpose it is sufficient to remember that it was because of his great generosity that his history developed into the idea of the modern Santa Claus.

In Europe today, December 6, the traditional date of the saint's death, is the day when parents give gifts to their children. In the United States, Christmas Day is the time for the arrival of gifts for the children, and others.

One of the most significant things about the symbol of gifts arriving by way of Saint Nicholas, or Santa Claus — which has come to us from the Dutch language — is the fact that he gives without any thought of receiving a gift in return. When parents give gifts to their children and tell them that "Santa brought them," they are giving anonymously. True giving is to do something for another, that you hope will make them happy, with no thought of getting something in return.

A passage in the New Testament points to this. "Thus, when you give alms, sound no trumpet before you, as the hypocrites do in the synagogues and in the streets, that they may be praised by men. Truly, I say to you, they have their reward. But when you give alms, do not let your left hand know what your right hand is doing, so that your alms may be in secret; and your Father who sees in secret will reward you" (Matthew 6:2-4). Alms refer to gifts given to help another. They are gifts given in love and concern for the one who is to receive them. They are not offered to win favor or love from the one to whom they are presented. Nor are they given to those who have earned them. They are symbols of grace, of unmerited love.

When Santa Claus is used in this fashion, as that mysterious gentleman who brings gifts under the cover of darkness, and in the giving makes all people happy, he is indeed a symbol of the meaning of Christian love. Think about it.

> *How silently, how silently, The Wondrous gift is given!*
> *So God imparts to human hearts The blessings of His heaven.*
> *No ear may hear His coming, But in this world of sin, Where meek souls will receive Him still, The dear Christ enters in.*

(From, "O Little Town Of Bethlehem" by Phillips Brooks, 1868)

The Candy Cane

One of the ways in which we are called to serve others is to be willing to help others in need. The Christmas symbol for this part of the Christian faith is the candy cane. The candy cane is in the shape of a shepherd's staff. We are told that this staff, or cane, served two purposes, in addition to being of help to the shepherd as he walked or climbed. When out in the fields or wilderness with the sheep, there were times when a little lamb would fall into a deep hole. With the hook end of his staff, the shepherd could extend his reach and save the animal that was under his protection. At night, the flock was returned to the safety of the home fold. The shepherd would stand at the entrance to the fenced enclosure, and with his staff extended, he would stop each sheep before it entered. In that way, he could check each of his sheep for wounds or bruises that needed immediate attention. If the animal was all right, he would raise the staff and let it pass. If not, then he would do whatever needed to be done to take care of the discovered situation. The candy cane reminds us that the Good Shepherd cares for each sheep in his fold. Jesus said of the good shepherd, ". . . the sheep hear his voice, and he calls his own sheep by name and leads them out" (John 10:3).

The application of this symbol can take many forms. It is during this season that extra support is raised for the needy of the community. But with that process, we seldom come to know, by name, the ones in need. Perhaps we could come closer to the example of Jesus if we would think about friends and loved ones who might have a special need and, after looking at our own resources, decide what we can do to help. This is not to minimize the care shown to the people of a community who are in need. This is just taking it a step further and

29

encouraging a more personal involvement. I am not suggesting that the person you help has to know who did what. Rather, I am encouraging you to encounter the experience simply on a one to one basis, not for your own glory but for the glory of God. Think about it.

> *Hail the heaven born Prince of Peace! Hail the Son of Righteousness!*
> *Light and life to all He brings, Risen with healing in His wings.*
> *Mild He lays His glory by, Born that man no more may die;*
> *Born to raise the sons of earth, Born to give them second birth,*
> *Hark! the herald angels sing, "Glory to the new born King."*

(By Charles Wesley, 1739)

Tinsel

The term *tinsel* comes from an ancient word that means "to adorn with metallic threads." Many a Christmas tree has silvery thin strips hanging from its branches. They are among the last things we add to the tree. It is then that we stand back and observe the finished product. Now is the time to relax and reflect.

There is an ancient legend that relates to the time shortly after the birth of Jesus. The setting for the story comes from Matthew:

> *Then Herod, when he saw that he had been tricked by the wise men, was in a furious rage, and he sent and killed all the male children in Bethlehem and in all that region who were two years old and under, according to the time which he had ascertained from the wise men (Matthew 2:16)*

From the gospel story, we know that the holy family was warned, in a dream (Matthew 2:13-15). The legend tells that when the family was traveling to Egypt, they came upon a cave late at night. It was very cold outside and so they decided to enter the cave for shelter from the winter and to rest. Within the cave, there was a spider who saw that the baby Jesus was cold and he wanted to help. But what could a spider do? He did the only thing he could do. He spun a web across the entrance to the cave to make a kind of curtain to help reduce the amount of cold air entering the cave. The cold of the night soon caused the web to become covered with frost and in the moonlight it did look like a white curtain. Shortly after this, so the story goes, the Roman soldiers came by in search of the family. They were just about to enter the cave when the captain saw the spider's web and, noticing its completeness, he said to his men, "Look, that web has not been broken. No one has entered here. Let us move on." Because the little spider did what it could do, God's will was fulfilled. There are some people who say that the silvery tinsel on the Christmas tree is a reminder of the shiny web of the spider that was covered with frost that cold winter night.

The story may not be true, but it does remind us of a special truth. We all have things that we can do in life. At the time, they may seem like little things. They may not even accomplish what we want them to do. But, when we do the best we can with whatever we have, then God has something from us with which he can work to fulfill his will. It is not necessary for us to know how our work may fit into God's plan. But if we are true to who we are and what we believe, we will be special instruments in the hands of God. Think about it.

God of our life, through all the circling years, We trust in Thee;
In all the past, through all our hopes and fears, Thy hand we see.
With each new day, when morning lifts the veil,
We own Thy mercies, Lord, which never fail.

God of the past, our times are in Thy hand; With us abide.
Lead us by faith to hope's true Promised Land; Be Thou our guide.
With Thee to bless, the darkness shines as light,
And faith's fair vision changes into sight.

God of the coming years, through paths unknown We follow Thee;
When we are strong, Lord, leave us not alone; Our refuge be.
Be Thou for us in life our Daily Bread,
Our heart's true Home when all our years have sped.

(By Hugh T. Kerr, 1916)

The Greeting Card And Letter

One activity that is very important during this season is the sending and receiving of Christmas cards and/or letters. Some people finish the task of selecting and sending their cards early in this time of preparation, and this is probably the best way to do it. But whether it is early or later, in the rush to get the mail out, we need to take care. I remember reading about one lady who, in the mad scramble of last minute Christmas shopping, bought a box of 50 identical greeting cards. Without bothering to read the verse, she hastily signed and addressed all but one of them. Several days after they had been mailed, she came across the one card that had not been sent and, up on looking at it, she was horrified to read: "This card is just to say a little gift is on the way." Rule number one in sending out cards: Make sure that the message and picture express what you want to express. For the practice to be meaningful for you, select a card that expresses what you feel about this season.

We need to communicate with the people we list as our friends. One unique feature of the timing of Christmas is the fact that it comes just one week before the start of a new year. For many people, the start of another year is the time when they take stock of life and resolve to try to improve on it. In these days of preparation for Christmas we would do well to let what we learn in preparation speak to what we might want to change in the year that is about to come. One worthy resolution is to desire greater communication with friends and loved ones who are far away.

In Christmas we celebrate God's actions which resulted in God communicating himself to individuals in the world. The name "Emmanuel," which is pronounced in this season, is the often forgotten other name for the Christ Child. "Behold, a virgin shall conceive and bear a son, and his name shall be called Emmanuel (which means, God with us)" (Matthew 1:23). Christmas is about being together and the greeting card and letter remind us of that meaning. Yet, as with all the symbols of the season and the meanings they contain, if we are willing to remember and reaffirm the important things of life that the season places before us, then we must also strive to carry those meanings into the rest of life. The seed must be allowed to grow. The dye must penetrate deep into the inner person and color everything we do. If we would make the spirit of Christmas last beyond Christmas Day, then we must become the personification of what we believe. Think about it.

Now to the Lord sing praises, All you within this place,
And with true love and brotherhood Each other now
embrace;
This holy tide of Christmas All others doth deface.
O tidings of comfort and joy, Comfort and joy;
O tidings of comfort and joy.

(From "God Rest Ye Merry, Gentlemen" English carol, eighteenth century)

The Christmas Gift (Wise Men)

Why do we give gifts at Christmas? The activity centers on the story of the wise men from the East, as recorded in chapter 2 of Matthew, verses 1-12. The author of this gospel makes no attempt to identify these men, other than the fact that they were wise men who came from the East. They are sometimes referred to as "Magi," a word denoting wisdom. They were said to be the keepers of sacred things. As such, they were looked upon as the learned ones among their people. In the biblical story, it is obvious that they were scholars, who had studied the stars and had interpreted certain facts based upon that knowledge. Because of that assessment, they came seeking a newborn king so that they could honor him. This they did by bringing gifts to him. There are several passages in the Old Testament which tell of kings bearing gifts. In Psalm 72:10-11 we read of other kings bringing gifts and serving the righteous King. And, in Isaiah 60:3, we read, "And nations shall come to your light, and kings to the brightness of your rising."

A gift is something that is given to another voluntarily and for which no payment is received or expected. It is a way we have of saying to another, "I love you" or "I think you are wonderful." God's ultimate gift to us is the giving of his son, Jesus. We remember that gift in one of the best known verses of the Bible, John 3:16, "For God so loved the world that he gave his only Son, that whoever believes in him should not perish but have eternal life." When we remember the giving of that great gift, it is appropriate that we should respond to God's love with expressions of our love. But how can we respond to God's love? Jesus taught that love of God and love of neighbor go hand in hand. (Cf. Matthew 22:37-40, John

35

13:34-35, 1 John 4:19). The giving of gifts to those we love is just one way open to us to show that we have learned of love from Jesus. Think about it.

Born Thy people to deliver, Born a child and yet a King,
Born to reign in us forever, Now Thy gracious Kingdom
bring.
By Thine own eternal Spirit Rule in all our hearts alone;
By Thine all sufficient merit Raise us to Thy glorious
throne.

(From "Come, Thou Long Expected Jesus"
by Charles Wesley, 1744)

The Wrapped Gift

One usual feature of gift giving at Christmas is the fact that all kinds of special gift wrapping paper is sold for our use in preparing the gifts for presentation to friends and loved ones. The Christmas tree, surrounded by beautifully wrapped presents, is often pictured on greeting cards and in advertisements calling attention to the coming event. The significance of the wrapped gift is often ignored, although it is experienced by many people, especially children. The wrapping around the gift helps us to know that "here is something special, just for me." But the special paper also says, "You must wait until Christmas before you unwrap it." It has been said that "anticipation is the essence of Christmas." Looking at the gift addressed to us, we can think of all the possibilities of what it might be. Some people will check its weight, or shake it to see if the sound will give a clue to the contents. We might review our "want" list and see if some object from that might resemble the size of the package. All this activity only heightens our anticipation and teaches us patience as we wait for the day to come. When the time is right, we will know what we have received.

The scriptures tell us that Christmas itself falls into that category. In the fullness of time, Jesus came. Paul wrote, "But when the time had fully come, God sent forth his Son, born of woman, born under the law, to redeem those who were under the law, so that we might receive adoption as sons" (Galatians 4:4, 5, also cf Mark 1:15). When the time was right, what God had promised became a reality for humanity. Part of the preparation for that world-changing event was that the people of Israel anticipated it. Christ means Messiah and Jesus was the Messiah that the Hebrew people expected. The woman at the well said to Jesus, "I know that Messiah is coming (he who is called Christ); when he comes, he will show us all things." Jesus said to her, "I who speak to you am he" (John 4:25, 26).

One thing that we need to do as we prepare for Christmas is to ask ourselves, "What do I want from Christmas?" If the only answer we can give is in terms of material things, then we are missing the whole point of what we celebrate. Christmas is a time to see life in a new way. It is the season that shows us that people can be kind to one another. It is the time when the world around us takes on new beauty, a shared beauty that is added to our surroundings to show forth the specialness of the season. It is an appropriate prelude to the start of a new year and its opportunity for a new beginning. Think about it.

> *Watchman, tell us of the night, What its signs of promise are:*
> *Traveler, o'er yon mountain's height, See that glory-beaming star!*
> *Watchman, doth its beauteous ray Aught of joy or hope foretell?*
> *Traveler, yes; it brings the day, Promised day of Israel.*

(By John Bowring, 1825)

The Poinsettia

Most of the symbols for the Christmas season come to us from what we call "The Old World." When the people of Europe came to our land, they brought with them their own individual customs and traditions. Many of these centered on religious celebrations, for freedom of religion was a major factor driving people to the "New World."

But not all of the Christmas symbols came from Europe. The poinsettia is a new world contribution to the season. In 1825, Joel Robert Poinsett of South Carolina, who had been appointed as the first American diplomat to Mexico, saw some flowers in that southern region called "flame flowers" or "flowers of the Holy Night" which were used as decorations in their festival Nativity processions. Dr. Poinsett happened to be a botanist. He sent cuttings back to America. About a century later, Paul Ecke of California came across the plant and began to cultivate it on a commercial scale.

The flower from Mexico is most interesting. Upon first view of the plant, one might assume that its flower is a bright red; but this is not true. Upon close examination, one will discover that there is a cluster of small yellow flowers in the center of the red (or pink or white) colored leaves. This leafy part of the plant, called bract, attracts the insects that then pollinate the almost-hidden tiny flowers.

One way that we can add meaning to the Christmas season is to think about the symbolism of what we see. This is especially true of the poinsettia. At first glance, we see only the red and green, the traditional Christmas colors. I have already referred to the meaning of green as the color of life. Red is also a color of life, but it is more specific. For the Hebrew people, the blood of a person or animal was believed to contain the essence of its life. When we speak of Jesus shedding his blood for us, we are referring to the fact that he died for our sins. Though he was without sin, he paid the price of what it means to be separated from God by sin. God is the source of true life. Sin cuts us off from God. Therefore, because of our sin, we are cut off from the source of true life. But Jesus took our place in death and by that, in the mystery of all ages, reunited the world with God. Through the essence of his life, including his death, we have new, eternal life. The red and the green belong together. But there is more. Hidden in the red is the symbol of gold, the symbol of precious things. Jesus came that we might have life and have it abundantly (John 10:10). We find that bountiful life as we search the scriptures and learn of Jesus who is the Way, the Truth and the Life (John 14:6). Think about it.

Come, Thou long expected Jesus, Born to set Thy people free;
From our fears and sins release us; Let us find our rest in Thee,
Israel's Strength and Consolation, Hope of all the earth Thou art;
Dear Desire of every nation, Joy of every longing heart.

(By Charles Wesley, 1744)

Circles

No other shape is more visible during the Advent season than the circle. We see it in wreaths, in halos on greeting cards, and in the spherical shape of many of the ornaments placed on the Christmas tree. Christmas itself is a circular event, for it comes around again every year.

The circle is used in many different ways in life. As a zero, it has no value by itself, but when added to another number, it has a tremendous effect. Five becomes 50 and then 500 and so on. The letter *O* can also change the meaning of many words. For example, add *O* to the word *God* and you have *good*. Another way of looking at this is to see that when we take God out of Good, what remains is zero. In our faith, we acknowledge that there is no real good without God. In James we read, "Every good endowment and every perfect gift is from above, coming down from the Father of lights with whom there is no variation or shadow due to change" (James 1:17).

The symbol *O* reminds us also of the need to reach out to others and to include them within the sphere of our own life. The letter *I* reminds us of the individual. That person can live a self-centered existence that has no room for others. But, in our faith, we believe that in order to live the full, abundant life, the *I* needs to be made inclusive and changed to *O*. To LIVE is to Love; and when LOVE is present, God is also present. "Beloved, let us love one another; for love is of God, and he who loves is born of God and knows God" (1 John 4:7).

Finally, remember that the symbol of the circle, having no end and no beginning, is also the symbol of eternity. What is given to us in the Christian faith, which began with the coming of the baby Jesus, is something that has meaning not only for this life, but for eternal life. We do not know what that life will be like; but we do believe that it will be life with God; and God is love and love is eternal. Life without God is hell; life with God is heaven. That is all we need to remember, and the circles of Christmas remind us of this truth. Think about it.

> O Love that wilt not let me go, I rest my weary soul
>   in Thee;
> I give Thee back the life I owe, That in Thine ocean
>   depths its flow May richer, fuller be.
> O Cross that liftest up my head; I dare not ask to fly
>   from Thee;
> I lay in dust life's glory dead, And from the ground there
>   blossoms red Life that shall endless be.

(By George Matheson, 1882)

Angels

Many Christmas trees are topped with a "Christmas" angel. The story of the birth of Jesus contains a massive invasion of angels. An angel appears to Joseph in a dream telling him to name Mary's baby Jesus, "for he will save his people from their sins" (Matthew 1:21). When the wise men came seeking the newborn king, they came to King Herod, assuming he would know where the event took place. He did not, but he asked the men to return and tell him, if they found such a child. They were warned in a dream not to return to Herod (Matthew 2:12). In the context of the other dreams in the Christmas story, we can assume that an angel was involved in the warning to the wise men. Because they did not return, King Herod sought to destroy Jesus by sending out his soldiers to kill all the babies they could find who were two years old or under. But that sorrowful event did not eliminate the Christ, for again Joseph was warned by an angel, in a dream (Matthew 2:13). Years later, when it was time for the Holy Family to return to Israel, the angel of the Lord appeared to Joseph in a dream (Matthew 2:19). In Luke, we are told an angel appeared to Zechariah, the father of John the Baptist who came to prepare the way for the Messiah (Luke 1:5-20). When Mary was informed about the coming birth of Jesus, it was an angel that carried the news to her (Luke 1:26-38). And, of course, who could forget the visit of the angels to the shepherds out in the field (Luke 2:8-14)?

The term *angel* means messenger. The purpose of the angel was to help God convey his message to the people who needed to hear about what God was doing. The angel, therefore, becomes an important symbol for the whole experience of Christmas. If we fail to hear the message and to remember what God has done for us, then this yearly celebration becomes nothing more than an excursion from reality. However, if the days of preparation and the event itself remind us of God's initiative, then all of life will be viewed with the overwhelming reality that God was — and is — active in our world. Just as Joseph and the wise men and Mary and the shepherds and Zechariah heard God's message and responded accordingly, so we also need to hear the message of this season and remember; and then apply what we believe to the living of everyday life. Think about it.

> *Hark! The herald angels sing, "Glory to the newborn King;*
> *Peace on earth, and mercy mild, God and sinners reconciled!"*
> *Joyful, all ye nations rise, Join the triumph of the skies;*
> *With angelic host proclaim, "Christ is born in Bethlehem!"*
> *Hark! The herald angels sing, "Glory to the newborn King."*
>
> (By Charles Wesley, 1739)

The Dove

There are many narratives related to animals at Christmas time. For example, there is a Russian legend that on the night of our Savior's birth barnyard animals helped to proclaim the good news. Therefore, it has been a tradition that on Christmas Eve the domestic animals are given an extra amount of food as a special "Holy Supper." In some countries, extra bird seed or pieces of suet are put out for the feathered friends. Barnyard animals are often included in the manger scene. Birds are often the subject of colorful ornaments that are added to the Christmas tree.

A major symbol of Christianity is the white, descending dove. This is because, on several occasions, the gospel story speaks of the Spirit of God coming upon Jesus "like a dove" (Matthew 3:16, Mark 1:10, Luke 3:22, John 1:32). The dove is also pictured with the olive branch in its mouth as a symbol of peace, from the story of Noah and the flood (Genesis 8:8-12). For both reasons, the dove is an appropriate Christmas symbol. The second name for the Christ, "Emmanuel" (which means God with us — Matthew 1:23) reminds us of a major part of the reason why Jesus came: namely, to bring God's spirit into life. The second reason for his coming is to reconcile God and humankind. That is, he came to bring peace.

The Spirit of God is essential for the living of the Christian life. We cannot see God the Father. As John wrote, "No one has ever seen God; the only Son, who is in the bosom of the Father, he has made him known" (John 1:18). And Jesus said, "He who has seen me has seen the Father" (John 14:9). But Jesus is no longer with us in bodily form. He has ascended to the Father. Therefore, whatever we experience in our relationship with God and with Jesus is the work of the Holy

Spirit, the Counselor. Of this Holy Spirit, Jesus said, "whom the Father will send in my name, he will teach you all things, and bring to your remembrance all that I have said to you. Peace I leave with you; my peace I give to you; not as the world gives do I give to you. Let not your hearts be troubled, neither let them be afraid" (John 14:26-27).

We need the symbol of the dove to remind us that God is always present in his Spirit, to teach us and guide us and comfort us. During the preparations for Christmas, we need to set aside some quiet times when we can let that Holy Spirit flow over us and through us to give us the peace that the world can neither give nor take away. Think about it.

> *Holy Spirit, Truth divine, Dawn upon this soul of mine;*
> *Word of God, and inward Light, Wake my spirit, clear my sight.*
> *Holy Spirit, Love divine, Glow within this heart of mine;*
> *Kindle every high desire; Perish self in Thy pure fire.*
> *Holy Spirit, Power divine, Fill and nerve this will of mine;*
> *By Thee may I strongly live, Bravely bear, and nobly strive.*
> *Holy Spirit, Right divine, King within my conscience reign;*
> *Be my Law, and I shall be Firmly bound, forever free.*

(By Samuel Longfellow, 1864)

The Shepherds

There are numerous people who were a part of the first Christmas. Many we know by name: Mary, Joseph, King Herod, Zechariah, Elizabeth, John. Others come to us as a group: the wise men and the shepherds. Tradition has given names to the wise men (Melchior, Gaspar or Caspar, Balthasar). They were important men and it is fitting that history should seek to name them. But such is not so with the shepherds out in the fields. We have no idea who they were. Yet, they come closer to representing most of us. As Paul said of the early Christians, "For consider your call, brethren; not many of you were wise according to worldly standards, not many were powerful, not many were of noble birth; but God chose what is foolish in the world to shame the wise, God chose what is weak in the world to shame the strong, God chose what is low and despised in the world, even things that are not, to bring to nothing things that are, so that no human being might boast in the presence of God. He is the source of your life in Christ Jesus, whom God made our wisdom, our righteousness and sanctification and redemption" (1 Corinthians 1:26-30).

What can we learn from the shepherds? First, they were not seeking a new king. They were busy doing their job. But God took the initiative with them and sent them a special messenger. God broke into their common ordinary night. Once that happened, they responded. "... The shepherds said to one another, 'Let us go over to Bethlehem and see this thing that has happened, which the Lord has made known to us' " (Luke 2:15). They put the message to the test, "And the shepherds returned, glorifying and praising God for all they had heard and seen, as it had been told them" (Luke 2:20).

It is not good enough to just hear the message of the season. The new life that is offered in Christ Jesus needs to

47

be given serious consideration and put to the test. As someone once said, "Faith is to believe in what you cannot see and
the reward of that faith is to see what you believe." For example, will loving your enemies work? It is really the only way
to get rid of them. If an enemy can become a friend, then he
or she is no longer an enemy. Think about it.

*Angels, from the realm of glory, Wing your flight o'er
all the earth;*
*Ye who sang creation's story, Now proclaim Messiah's
birth:*
*Come and worship, Come and worship, Worship Christ
the newborn King!*
*Shepherds, in the fields abiding, Watching o'er your
flocks by night;*
*God with man is now residing, Yonder shines the infant
Light:*
*Come and worship, Come and worship, Worship Christ
the newborn King!*
*Sages, leave your contemplations, Brighter visions beam
afar;*
*Seek the great Desire of nations; Ye have seen His natal
star:*
*Come and worship, Come and worship, Worship Christ
the newborn King!*

(By James Montgomery, 1816)

Ornaments

We are accustomed to seeing things hanging on a tree. We look forward to the harvest when the fruit trees provide us with many delicious and healthy things to eat. In the fall, in many parts of our country, we find great pleasure in watching the leaves change colors and we, in memory or on film, strive to capture the brilliance and compare it to other falls. Also, campers and historians will tell us of a special activity of people who live or have lived in the out-of-doors. To protect precious food, they tied it high in a tree so that it could not be reached by most of the wild animals. So it is natural that food was among the first objects to find its way onto the Christmas tree. We are told that the earliest account of such a decoration is to be found in the diary of a traveler to Strasbourg, in Alsace — a former province in eastern France. He wrote in 1605 about seeing a Christmas tree decorated with cookies and candies.

When a Christmas tree is decorated with its numerous ornaments and lights, we stand back and find great pleasure in simply looking at the spectacle. As the years move along, the ornaments of the past return to sight and remind us of bygone Christmases. Each year ornaments are created to serve as a token reminder of a young couple's first Christmas together, or the first Christmas in the life of a child. Today also we have ornaments in motion that depict winter scenes of skating or sledding, or other holiday events of the past. Soon the tree is covered with symbols of our faith, or of things to remember, or sights to enjoy. It is a wonderful tradition, for it speaks to the inner spirit. And that is what we must remember at the Christmas season. All the beauty and sparkle and color will remain as just so much "show" if it fails to inspire us to create good memories and to take within our heart and soul the love of God and of one another.

It is common to feel the wonderfulness of life during the season of Christmas. This is the time to bring into our heart and soul the spirit that will make life beautiful. The attributes that help to form life as God intended it to be are, according to Paul, "... love, joy, peace, patience, kindness, goodness, faithfulness, gentleness, self-control ..." (Galatians 6:22-23). These are the fruit of the Spirit. In these days, seek these ways. Think about it.

God rest ye merry, gentlemen, Let nothing you dismay,
Remember Christ our Saviour Was born on Christmas
    Day;
To save us all from Satan's power When we were gone
    astray.
O tidings of comfort and joy, Comfort and joy;
    O tidings of comfort and joy.
Now to the Lord sing praises, All you within this place,
And with true love and brotherhood Each other now
    embrace;
This holy tide of Christmas All other doth deface.
O tidings of comfort and joy, Comfort and joy.
    O tidings of comfort and joy.

    (English traditional)

The Bells

During the Advent season it is not unusual to hear the song, "Jingle Bells." The jingling bells carry us back to the time of winter sleigh rides, behind a team of prancing ponies and dashing o'er the snow. But bells are used in other ways than just to jingle. The church bell calls us to worship. The dinner bell tells us that the meal is ready to be served. The bell was used to tell time in that era before the pocket or wrist watch. It was also used to mark a special time. In Norway, for example, all work is to stop at 4:00 p.m. on Christmas Eve so that the celebration of Christmas may begin. The signal is given by the church bells ringing across the land.

The ringing of a great bell, heard by all the community, reminds us of the inclusiveness of Christmas. One of the thrilling things about the Advent season is that it affects everyone. We cannot control how people will react to the inclusion, but part of the pull of the season is the fact that everyone is drawn into it, in some way.

We see that involvement even in the first Christmas story. There were three wise men. A multitude of a heavenly host was sent to the shepherds out in the field. Mary and Joseph had to spend the night in a stable because the city of Bethlehem was overcrowded with people.

Many of the teachings of Jesus came to us in the plural form. For example, "By this all men will know that you are my disciples, if you have love for one another" (John 13:35). And the Lord's Prayer was given in response to the question, "Lord, teach us to pray" (Luke 11:1).

Faith is a very private matter; but the result of that faith must reach out to influence our life with the lives around us. Christmas is not a private celebration. It brings family and friends together. It causes quarreling factions to set a truce for the season, for we cannot honor the Prince of Peace with hatred toward others. The call of Good News is for all the people.

As we plan for the events of the season, we should include times of fellowship with others. The sending of Christmas cards and the giving of gifts to people outside the immediate family is in response to that urge. We need to hear the Christmas bells ringing in our heart and soul and calling us into the community that surrounds us and adds so much to the meaning of being alive. Think about it.

I heard the bells on Christmas Day
Their old, familiar carols play,
And wild and sweet The word repeat
Of peace on earth, good-will to men!

Then pealed the bells more loud and deep:
"God is not dead; nor doth He sleep!
The Wrong shall fail,
The Right prevail,
With peace on earth, good-will to men."

(By Henry Wadsworth Longfellow, 1863)

Music

The feeding of the inner person can also be accomplished by using music. As the day of Christmas draws near, the vibrant sounds of Christmas music can be heard everywhere. As the Psalmist instructed the ancient people of God, so his words ring true again: "Make a joyful noise to the Lord, all the lands! ... Know that the Lord is God! It is he that made us, and we are his; ... For the Lord is good; his steadfast love endures for ever, and his faithfulness to all generations" (Psalm 100:1, 3, 5).

The word *Noel* has become a term that is synonymous with Christmas. It is derived from the French language where it meant *birth*. But the word is also defined, when not capitalized, as a Christmas carol. A carol is a song used to celebrate. It is assumed that it is derived from the Greek word *choros,* which means a dance. Because Christmas is a time of great celebration, joyful song is a natural part of what we experience.

Music is another symbol for continuity, for a universal continuity. There are some people who believe that Saint Francis, who brought the teachings of the Church into the everyday lives of the common people, may have created some of the earliest carols. Many of our current carols were produced in the eighteenth and nineteenth centuries, as were many great Christmas classics, like the *Messiah* with its magnificent "Hallelujah Chorus," by George Frederick Handel.

All of this is to remind us that when we prepare for our Christmas season, we are taking our place with many generations past who found inspiration and beauty, faith and joy, in taking part in honoring what God has done for us in Christ Jesus. In like fashion, we need to remember that what we do in these days helps to set the tone for the coming years for the children in our family and in the families of our community.

There is a story in the Old Testament that tells about the time when the people of Israel came into their new land. Under the leadership of Joshua, the people were instructed to make a pile of 12 stones, one for each tribe. "And he said to the people of Israel, 'When your children ask their fathers in time to come, "What do these stones mean?" then you shall let your children know, "Israel passed over this Jordan on dry ground." ... so that all the peoples of the earth may know that the hand of the Lord is mighty ...' " (Joshua 4:21-24). In a like fashion, we need to help our children understand what the symbols of Advent and Christmas mean to us and what they meant to our ancestors. Think about it.

> *A thousand years have come and gone, And near a thousand more,*
> *Since happier light from heaven shone Than ever shone before;*
> *And in the hearts of old and young A joy most joyful stirred,*
> *That sent such news from tongue to tongue As ears had never heard.*

(By Thomas Toke Lynch, 1868)

The Holly

Many symbols of the Christmas season come to us from pre-Christian times. In the medieval days, people were afraid of anything that they could not understand. They also assumed that the hostile forces of nature were the work of demonic spirits. In that setting, all kinds of talismans came into existence. One of these was the holly. Since it remains green through the winter months, it was apparently assumed that it had special powers to withstand the forces of winter. In that ancient time, the howling winter winds would sound like the wailing of some evil spirit. Anything that would have magical powers against such mysterious things would be welcomed. Even before the time of Jesus, the Druids considered the holly to be sacred. That meant, for them, that the plant was inhabited by good spirits. Therefore, bringing a branch into the house for the wintertime would bring a good spirit into the home in the hope that it would be a shield against the hardship of winter.

Most people today have set aside the old superstitions of the past. However, this should not result in completely ignoring the symbolism of an ancient charm. Therefore, one task, given to us all in the season of Advent, is to let the symbols that surround us speak to us. As in the past, people gave new meaning to old symbols, so also today, we need to search for our own new meanings.

What meaning can we give to the holly? We have already thought about the symbol of being "ever green" as a reminder of everlasting life. We also hope that the ongoing life will be a life of quality, not just quantity, and the rich, dark green of the holly represents that hope. But life in this world is not without its hardship. Some people would even say that difficulties are necessary if life is to grow properly. As Paul wrote, "More than that, we rejoice in our sufferings, knowing that suffering produces endurance, and endurance produces character, and character produces hope, and hope does not disappoint us, because God's love has been poured into our hearts through the Holy Spirit which has been given to us" (Romans 5:3-5). The sharp points on the holly leaf symbolize the hardship and suffering that life contains. Think about it.

There is an old English carol that has captured the symbolism of the holly:

The holly and the ivy,
Now they are full well grown,
Of all the trees that are in the woods,
The holly bears the crown.

The holly bears a blossom
As white as the lily flower,
And Mary bore sweet Jesus Christ
To be our sweet saviour.

The holly bears a berry
As red as any blood,
And Mary bore sweet Jesus Christ
To do poor sinners good.

The holly bears a prickle
As sharp as any thorn,
And Mary bore sweet Jesus Christ
On Christmas day in the morn.

The holly bears a bark
As bitter as any gall,
And Mary bore sweet Jesus Christ
For to redeem us all.

The holly and the ivy,
Now both are full well grown,
Of all the trees that are in the wood,
The holly bears the crown.

(Medieval English carol)

Gold

Advent is a season of many colors. The traditional red and green are seen everywhere; and so is the color gold. Gold is a precious metal and so it was fitting that one of the wise men brought gold to the Holy Family as his gift to the newborn King (Matthew 2:11).

The Bible has much to say to us about the symbolism of gold. In the Old Testament, it was the metal used to form the golden calf that became a substitute for the worship of the one true God (Exodus 32). This was displeasing to Almighty God for it symbolized idolatry, the worship of false gods.

However, gold can also be used to represent the best in life, materially speaking. But again there is a danger. There is more to life than material things, and so, Proverbs advises us that there is something more precious than gold: "Take my instruction instead of silver, and knowledge rather than choice gold; for wisdom is better than jewels, and all that you may desire cannot compare with her" (Proverbs 8:10, 11). Yet, the Bible does offer the image of gold as a symbol for the best that we are to search after. In Revelation we read: "Therefore, I counsel you to buy from me gold refined by fire, that you may be rich ... Those whom I love, I reprove and chasten; so be zealous and repent. Behold, I stand at the door and knock; if any one hears my voice and opens the door, I will come in to him and eat with him, and he with me" (Revelation 3:18-20).

Gold needs to go through a process of refining that results in a purer metal. Peter used that symbolism to encourage us in times of hardship. After writing about being born anew to a living hope through the resurrection of Jesus to an inheritance that is imperishable, undefiled, and unfading, he stated, "In this you rejoice, though now for a little while you may have to suffer various trials, so that the genuineness of your faith, more precious than gold which though perishable is tested by fire, may redound to praise and glory and honor at the revelation of Jesus Christ. Without having seen him you love him; though you do not now see him you believe in him and rejoice with unutterable and exalted joy. As the outcome of your faith you obtain the salvation of your souls" (1 Peter 1:6-9).

It is important that we remember the resurrection of Jesus at this Advent season. It is because of his rising from the dead that we celebrate his birth. Jesus was more than a good person, or a good teacher, or a sinless man. He was God with us and through his life and death and resurrection we can have fellowship with the one true eternal God. That is life's most precious gift. Think about it.

> *Born a King on Bethlehem's plain, Gold I bring to crown Him again,*
> *King for ever, ceasing never Over us all to reign.*
> *O star of wonder, star of night, Star with royal beauty bright,*
> *Westward leading, still proceeding, Guide us to thy perfect Light.*

> (From "We Three Kings" by John H. Hopkins, Jr., 1857)

The Christmas Stocking

Isn't it interesting to see all the traditions of the season and see how often people do them without any thought to the meaning of the actions? A case in point is the hanging of the Christmas stocking above the fireplace or in another location, if a mantle is not available. What a strange thing to do.

The reason for this practice goes back to the legend of Saint Nicholas. The story tells of a nobleman who had a wife and three daughters. In time, his wife died and the nobleman lost his way and wasted his fortune. Soon the family was forced to live in poverty. Eventually, his three daughters grew up and wanted to get married, but the poor father had nothing left for a dowry — a sum of money or some valuable property that, by tradition, was brought by the bride to her husband at marriage. Saint Nicholas lived in that area and, having devoted his life to helping others, when he heard about their plight, he wanted to do something. He went to their cottage one night, and looking in through a hole in the wall, he saw that the three sisters, having washed their clothes, had hung them by the fireplace to dry. Saint Nicholas hit upon a plan to leave the money for the young women. He climbed up on the roof, carefully dropped three bags of money down the chimney and was able to have one bag land in each girl's stocking. The father heard the commotion on the roof and looked out just in time to see Saint Nicholas disappear into the darkness. Because of Saint Nicholas' goodness, the father's problem was solved.

Here is a symbol from the past that speaks to the wonderful quality in life of helping someone who is in need when we can do something to help. Within the world today there are many problems that we hear about or experience, and we shake our heads in despair, saying, "What can we do about it?" The answer we feel rising within us is, "Nothing!"

To go through life with that feeling is to miss a major joy in life. Every day, we come upon people who need help. It may be as simple as holding a door open for a person who is leaving a store with an armful of packages. Or it might be as big as the anonymous gift of Saint Nicholas to help a person have a new life. The first step is the willingness to do something. Then we look at the need and at our resources and we do what we can. Being sensitive to the needs of the people in your own extended family, including your religious community, is a good place to start.

As Paul reminded the people of Ephesus, "In all things I have shown you that by so toiling one must help the weak, remembering the words of the Lord Jesus, how he said, 'It is more blessed to give than to receive' " (Acts 20:35). He also wrote, "If any one does not provide for his relatives, and especially for his own family, he has disowned the faith and is worse than an unbeliever" (1 Timothy 5:8). And "So then, as we have opportunity, let us do good to all men, and especially to those who are of the household of faith" (Galatians 6:10). Think about it.

We are not daily beggars That beg from door to door,
But we are neighbor's children Whom you have seen
    before.
Love and joy come to you, And to you your wassail too,
And God bless you and send you a happy new year,
And God send you a happy new year.

(From "Wassail Song," English traditional)

(Note: The word *wassail* is an old Anglo-Saxon word from *waes hael* which means "be well." In ancient times, in the dead of winter, a procession from the village would visit the apple orchards and sprinkle a "waes hael" mixture on the tree in an attempt to insure a good crop come the spring and harvest time. Eventually, the procession became a part of the Christmas tradition as groups of carolers would go from house to house to wish the residents good cheer and a merry Christmas. Often these groups would be invited into the house for refreshments, including a glass of punch from the Wassail Bowl.)

Joseph And Mary

The earthly parents of Jesus were simple folk. Very little is known about Joseph. We assume he was a carpenter since Jesus was referred to as the son of the carpenter (Matthew 13:55). The genealogies in the New Testament trace his family tree back to King David. Other than that, all we can assume about him is that he was a man of faith in God, who was the protector and provider for the Christ child in his infant years. He also was responsible for the meaningful name of "Jesus" that was given to this baby (Matthew 1:20, 21). Jesus is the English form of the Latin translation of the Greek. However, the original Hebrew form was Joshua which means "God is salvation," or "God will save it." It was Joseph who took Jesus and Mary to Egypt so that King Herod could not get to him (Matthew 2:13-23). Joseph was essential to the life of Jesus. He did what he felt he needed to do to protect and provide for his family. He did not do it for special glory. He simply did what had to be done.

Of Mary, we have more information. The Magnificat, recorded in Luke 1:46-55, allows us to know her thoughts before the birth of Jesus. She saw herself as a simple servant of God. She pondered the early events in her child's life, keeping them in her heart (Luke 2:19-51). She was present with him at the time of his first miracle, at the wedding feast at Cana (John 2:1-11). And she was with him at his death (John 19:26-27). There were times when she did not understand what Jesus was doing or why he did it (Luke 2:41-48).

We are like Joseph and Mary. Most of the people we know — including ourselves — are common, ordinary people. We hope that our life will count for something, but it is not necessarily our task to say what that specialness will be. It may be, as with Joseph, that our importance will center on what we can do for someone else. By helping that person survive and strive, we may be assisting God to accomplish his will. Like Mary, we may not always understand how what we do will fulfill God's purpose. Perhaps all we can say is, "He who is mighty has done (and will do) great things for me (and through me), and holy is his name." Think about it.

> *Silent night! holy night! All is calm, all is bright,*
> *Round yon Virgin Mother and Child! Holy Infant, so*
> *tender and mild,*
> *Sleep in heavenly peace, Sleep in heavenly peace.*
>
> *Silent night! holy night! Son of God, love's pure light*
> *Radiant beams from Thy holy face, With the dawn of*
> *redeeming grace,*
> *Jesus, Lord, at Thy birth, Jesus, Lord, at Thy birth.*

(By Joseph Mohr, 1818)

The Infant Jesus

The purpose of our preparation during Advent is to celebrate and seek to understand the birth of Jesus to Mary, with the help of Joseph. No words were spoken that night by the Son of God. No miracle or signs were given by him whom we claim is Emmanuel, God with us. The sign to the shepherds was that he would be wrapped in swaddling cloths and lying in a manger. The swaddling cloths were strips of linen, or other material, wound about a newborn baby. This was a common practice. What was not so common was to find such a baby, lying in a manger, which was a trough, or box, used for the feeding of the cattle.

The baby Jesus, at the time of his birth, did not even have his own bed. Imagine the cattle, coming to eat, and finding not food but a newborn baby. Imagine shepherds, coming to see the Savior, who is Christ the Lord, and finding such a humble setting. It is not what would be expected.

In like fashion, we must approach our life with God with eyes open to the unexpected. God works in wondrous ways. He works in mysterious ways. He often uses common, ordinary things to convey his message. "For my thoughts are not your thoughts, neither are your ways my ways, says the Lord" (Isaiah 55:8). We need to pray to God to help us see things in his light. We need to ask for guidance so that we can make the right interpretations of the signs and symbols that are around us. We need to seek that sensitivity that will enable us to see God in every event and every person as we meet them in our journey through life. Think about it.

*What child is this, who, laid to rest, On Mary's lap is
sleeping?*

*Whom angels greet with anthems sweet, While shepherds
watch are keeping?*

*This, this is Christ the King, Whom shepherds guard and
angels sing!*

*Haste, haste to bring him laud, The Babe, the Son of
Mary!*

*Why lies he in such mean estate, Where ox and ass are
feeding?*

*Good Christian, fear, for sinners here The silent Word
is pleading.*

*Nails, spear, shall pierce him through, The cross be
borne for me, for you.*

*Hail, hail, the Word made flesh, The Babe, the Son of
Mary!*

*So bring him incense, gold and myrrh; Come, peasant,
king, to own him.*

*The King of kings, salvation brings; Let loving hearts
enthrone him.*

Raise, raise the song on high! The virgin sings her lullaby.

Joy, joy, for Christ is born, The Babe, the Son of Mary!

(By William Chatterton Dix, 1861)

December 25th

You may have heard that it is not known on what day of the year Jesus was born. This being so, we may ask, "Why was December 25 chosen?"

Before the time of Jesus, ancient scientists had observed that, around December 22, the sun was at its lowest point in the sky. At that time, there was no apparent northward or southward movement. It is the shortest daylight time of the year. People then believed that the gods controlled all things but they needed the help of humans to assure that the sun would rise in the sky and warmer weather would return. This help came in the form of magic and religious celebrations. According to the *Encyclopedia Britannica,* December 25 was a pagan festival in Rome, chosen in A.D. 274 by the emperor Aurelian as the birthday of the unconquered sun. That is, it was a pagan celebration to worship the sun. Around A.D. 336, the church of Rome declared that December 25 would be the day to commemorate the birthday of Jesus, the son of righteousness. This was one way that the Christian faith worked to supplant the pagan religions. It took over prevailing forms of pagan worship and transformed them.

Today, it is common to hear concern expressed about the fact that too many people have forgotten who and what is at the center of the Christmas celebration. We live in a pluralistic society. New forms of paganism are present everywhere. If we want to counteract the present condition, what can we do?

The answer must be found in our personal response to the opportunities of the season. What we do and how we commemorate this event must reflect what we believe about the Son of God. In the words of Paul, "Do not be conformed to this world but be transformed by the renewal of your minds, that you may prove what is the will of God, what is good and acceptable and perfect" (Romans 12:2). Think about it.

It came upon the midnight clear, That glorious song
* of old,*
From angels bending near the earth To touch their harps
* of gold;*
"Peace on the earth, good-will to men, From heaven's all
* gracious King":*
The world in solemn stillness lay, To hear the angels sing.

For lo, the days are hastening on, By prophet bards
* foretold,*
When with the ever circling years Comes round the age
* of gold;*
When peace shall over all the earth its ancient splendors
* fling,*
And the whole world give back the song Which now the
* angels sing.*

(By Edmund H. Sears, 1850)

Index To Poems, Hymns And Carols

Bibliography

Chalmer, Irena, *The Great American Christmas Almanac*. New York, Viking Studio Books, 1988.

Del Re, Gerard and Patricia, *The Christmas Almanack*. New York, Doubleday and Company, Inc., 1979.

Hottes, Alfred Carl, *1001 Christmas Facts and Fancies*. New York, A. T. De La Mare Company, Inc., 1938.

Krythe, Maymie R., *All About Christmas*. New York, Harpers and Brothers, 1954.

The Whole Christmas Catalogue. Revised by Barbara Radcliffe Rodgers, Los Angeles, Price Stern Sloan, 1986.

Check your local library for many other good books dealing with the meaning, tradition and symbolism of Christmas.